BASIC ISSUES
A Christian View

Contents

ISSUE 1	**Family and Friends**	4
ISSUE 2	**Marriage**	8
ISSUE 3	**Children — or not**	12
ISSUE 4	**Prejudice**	16
ISSUE 5	**Handicap**	20
ISSUE 6	**Pain, Old Age and Death**	24
ISSUE 7	**Housing and Healing the World**	28
ISSUE 8	**Feeding and Educating the World**	32
ISSUE 9	**Work and Unemployment**	36
ISSUE 10	**Leisure**	40
ISSUE 11	**Money and Possessions**	44
ISSUE 12	**Addiction**	48
ISSUE 13	**Evil, Crime and the Law**	52
ISSUE 14	**Politics and International Affairs**	56
ISSUE 15	**Environment**	60
	Index	64

Clare Richards
Nelson

Thomas Nelson and Sons Ltd
Nelson House Mayfield Road
Walton-on-Thames Surrey
KT12 5PL UK

Thomas Nelson Australia
102 Dodds Street
South Melbourne
Victoria 3205 Australia

Nelson Canada
1120 Birchmount Road
Scarborough Ontario
M1K 5G4 Canada

© Clare Richards 1990

First published by Blackie and Son Ltd 1990
ISBN 0-216-92893-1

This edition published by Thomas Nelson and Sons Ltd 1993

I(T)P Thomas Nelson is an International Thomson Publishing Company

I(T)P is used under licence

ISBN 0-17-437105-5
NPN 9 8 7 6 5

All rights reserved. No part of this publication may be reproduced, copied or transmitted save with written permission or in accordance with the provisions of the Copyright, Design and Patents Act 1988, or under the terms of any licence permitting limited copying issued by the Copyright Licensing Agency, 90 Tottenham Court Road, London W1P 9HE.

Any person who does any unauthorised act in relation to this publication may be liable to criminal prosecution and civil claims for damages.

Printed in China

Acknowledgements

The author and publishers are grateful to the following for permission to use copyright material:

Photographs
Chinelo Dieke cover (top left)
John Fisher pages 5, 6, 16, 28 (left), 33, 41 (bottom), 51
Clare Richards pages 7, 20, 28 (right), 32, 40 (right), 44, 45 (left), 59
R. Harrowven cover (top right & bottom left), pages 8, 24 (top left & right), 30, 41 (top)
Mike Carey pages 9, 10
The Cameo Photographic Studio page 12
J. Marquart page 13
The Guardian and Manchester Evening News page 14
L'Arche page 21
UNRWA pages 22 (Emile Andria), 23, 34 (top) (M. Nasr), 38, 55 (M. Nasr)
USPG (G. Grace) cover (bottom right), page 24 (bottom left)
St. John Ambulance page 24 (bottom right)
R. Milward page 25 (top), 40 (left)
Eastern Daily Press page 25 (bottom)
Adrian Bell page 34 (bottom)
Sister Claudia page 35
Society of African Missions page 36 (top)
SVD Fathers page 36 (bottom)
Barnaby's Picture Library page 45 (right)
E. Polednik page 48
Father Dunstan Thill page 50
Andy Worman page 56
Ministry of Defence page 57
Pam Tregunna pages 60, 63
The Telegraph Colour Library page 61

Illustrations
Dorothy Hamilton pages 4, 8, 17, 37, 53
Clare Richards pages 19, 30, 31, 32, 43, 49 (top), 62, 63
Julie Hogan page 26
Nick Raven page 42
Health Education Authority page 49 (bottom)
Lucy Clibban page 52

Introduction

This is a book for students who follow a Religious Studies programme in the 4th or 5th year, but who may not be taking an examination.

Until about 1900, most people in Britain would have been members of a Christian church.

Who are the Christians?
Christians are followers of Jesus, a Jew of the 1st century. They call him The Christ, that is, the one chosen by God.

His teaching is contained in the four Gospels of the Bible. Over the ages, Christians have broken into thousands of denominations. But there are three main branches:
1 The Roman Catholic Church,
2 The Orthodox Church,
3 The Churches of the Protestant Reformation.

What are the issues?
The issues studied in this book are ones which affect your daily life.

There are *personal issues*—about your family, your relationships, and your work and leisure.

And there are *social and political issues*—about Prejudice, Addiction, Law.

Some of the issues are of *world importance*, like poverty and conservation.

This book looks at the basic beliefs shared by Christians of all three branches. It tells you what Christians think about family, social and world issues. You may not be a Christian yourself but you need to know how others think.

Tasks that should be done in a group are marked by the symbol **G** and tasks to be done by each of you individually are marked by the symbol **I**.

The biblical quotations are taken from the *Good News Bible*. An index of biblical references is given below.

Index of Biblical References

Genesis		Matthew		15:1–7	55
1:1–2:4	43, 61	6:1–4	46	15:11–32	54
1:26	5	6:19–34	46	16:19–31	46
2:3	38, 42	6:26–29	38	23:32–41	55
6:9–7:23	63	Mark		Acts of the Apostles	
Exodus		6:31	42	2:44–47	21
20:9–10	42	8:4	33	1 Corinthians	
Deuteronomy		10:7–9	10	6:19–20	50
26:12	33	10:17–31	46	15:54–57	26
Psalms		10:43	38	Galations	
8	63	12:41–44	46	3:28	18
104	63	Luke		Ephesians	
Proverbs		5:29–32	55	6:5–8	38
19:15	38	6:27–38	55		
23:22	5	9:51–56	55		
23:29	50	10:38–42	38		
24:3	5	12:13–21	46		

ISSUE 1
Family and Friends

We all belong to a family. There are different family patterns. Which is yours?

Match the pictures with the descriptions below.

1 **Nuclear family:** Usually small family group of parents and children. Often better off than other groups.
2 **Extended family:** Made up of several generations living together.
3 **Wider family:** Families, students, sick or elderly people, homosexual partners who share accommodation or live as a community.
4 **One-parent family:** Children living with one parent (unmarried, widowed, divorced or deserted).
One child in eight in England and Wales.
5 **Reconstituted family:** Families where one or both parents have divorced and remarried. Children in these remarriages have step-parents.
6 **Single people:** Unmarried, widowed, divorced or deserted people.

What do Christians Think?

Most Christians believe that the human race is the best part of creation.

They have adopted the Jewish story of creation. It shows that people are God's masterpiece. People are images of God himself.

> "Then God said, 'And now we will make human beings, they will be like us and resemble us. They will have power over the fish, the birds, and all animals.'"
> Genesis 1:26

Christians look above all at the life of **Jesus** to find their model for friendship and family life. Jesus did not preach about the *ideal* family. He taught, by words and example, that *all* relationships are important. They should be loving, caring and forgiving.

> Christians agree that human society is founded on the rock of family life.
>
> "The family is the foundation of society."
> Roman Catholic Church. Vatican II
>
> "Listen to your father; without him you would not exist. When your mother is old, show her your appreciation." Proverbs 23:22
>
> "Homes are built on the foundation of wisdom and understanding." Proverbs 24:3

Dear Clare...

If you have a problem—share it. You'll feel much better. Write to Clare.

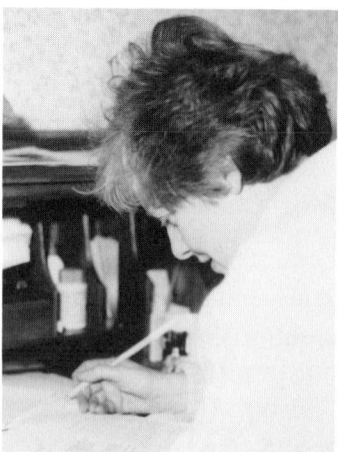

Idol talk

My 14-year-old daughter talks all the time about a girl who, at 16, is in the county athletic team and starring in the school play. She idolises this girl but shows no interest in boys and is rather shy. I'm worried.

Why can't he be serious?

I really like my boyfriend, and we have a good laugh together, but I wish he could be serious some of the time. If I start to talk about the future or tell him I love him, all he can do is crack another joke. How do I know if he loves me?

Family feud

My husband's mother lives with us. She's always telling the children off and criticising me for being "too soft" with them. It's making family life a nightmare.

Quarrelling kids

What can I do to stop my teenage children from quarrelling? Although they get on quite well sometimes, they do have violent arguments. My 17-year old son usually starts it by teasing his sister.

Feeling lonely

I recently found my 14-year old daughter in tears in her bedroom. Eventually she told me she felt all alone in the world. What can I do to help her?

I'm on the side lines

My girlfriend is a great sports fanatic. Most weekends she plays squash and goes swimming. I spend a lot of time hanging around waiting for her. I have never been interested in sport. I'm not really sure why she likes me.

Respect for others

I really like this girl. But she keeps laughing at my Mum, behind her back, because she goes to church. I respect Mum's views and wonder if I should stop seeing my girlfriend.

Worried about Dad

My parents have parted. I live with Dad and my new stepmum. My stepbrother and Dad keep shouting at each other. It's getting me down and making my Dad so unhappy. What can I do?

TASKS

1 ▶ Select two of these letters and write a reply to them.

2 ▶ Use a tape recorder to make a "radio phone-in" programme.
Choose 1 a programme presenter
2 an agony aunt and an agony uncle.

The rest of the group phone in the letters on this page.
(Note: Think up your replies before going on tape.)

▶ Write a letter yourself to an agony aunt.

Work for your Folder

EASTENDERS Neighbours Coronation Street BROOKSIDE DALLAS Home and Away

THINK ABOUT IT
▶ Which character is most like YOU? Why?
▶ Which qualities would you like to possess?

Jesus taught that relationships are demanding. It is difficult to love and accept others. He challenged people to be as generous and FORGIVING as God is. God, he said, forgives everything.

1 Choose your favourite soap opera.
2 Make a list of all the characters you can remember.
3 Put the characters into families.

4 Look again at the six types of "family" on page 4. Put your soap-opera families into these six groups.
5 Choose six characters from your soap opera to receive the following titles:
   a The most likeable character
   b The most ruthless character
   c The most honest character
   d The most to be pitied
   e The loneliest character
   f The most generous character.

TASKS
▶ Choose an incident in a soap opera where characters fall out with each other.
▶ Did they make it up?
Why? Why not?
▶ Is there anything that you could never forgive?
Why? Why not?

ISSUE 1 FAMILY AND FRIENDS

ISSUE 2

Marriage

Love is:

Getting on well with people is not easy. What is real friendship? Someone once said, "Friendship is like money, easier made than kept."

TASK

1 ▶ Make two lists:
1 ten ways to keep a friend
2 ten ways to lose a friend.

Is there true love?

I want to know if there's such a thing as true love. This may sound ridiculous, but it's really worrying me. Next year I'm going to marry a wonderful man. He isn't perfect, of course, but neither am I. One of my traits is that I always think twice before I do anything, and I want to be totally sure. I love my fiancé, but it isn't a "cloud nine" kind of love. When we see each other, we're pleased but not ecstatically happy. Am I being silly thinking that you should only get married if you're besotted with each other? I don't want to get married and then find that I've denied us both something special. On the other hand, if it's all fiction and what we have is as good as it comes, then I want to work at it and make it as near-perfect as possible.

Tracy

TASKS

1 ▶ Write a reply to Tracy.
▶ Draw a cartoon "Friendship is . . . ."
▶ Draw a cartoon "Love is . . . ."

Love is . . . giving surprises

Wedding Bells

John and Fiona are getting married. They plan their future carefully. They have thought about:
- where to live
- wage-earning
- sharing housework
- each other's interests
- companionship
- having a family.

Wedding plans
Fiona and John decide to have a church wedding. Why marry in church? Fiona said:
- Because we are Christians. We want God's blessing.
- Because my parents want it in their church.
- Because I don't want a ceremony which is over in a few minutes.
- Because I like some traditions, and a church wedding is one of them.

TASKS

1 ▶ Peter and Polly decide on a registry office wedding. Give *four* reasons for their decision.

G ▶ List everything you need to do to plan a wedding:
for example, invitations; book church or registry office; flowers; reception....

▶ Plan out Fiona and John's wedding. Check details in a "Wedding Etiquette" book.

▶ Make a rough guess at the cost of the wedding you plan. Don't forget the reception.

What do Christians Think?

- Christians believe that marriage is sacred (a challenging, dynamic way of life).
- Christian couples make their marriage vows (promises) to one another. They usually do so "before God" in a religious ceremony. He is their witness.
- Christians have firm beliefs about the responsibilities of married people:
the marriage is with one partner only—this is called monogamy; marriage should be for life—"until death us do part"; sexual intercourse should only be between a married couple; many Christians say that one of the purposes of marriage is to have children.

> Jesus said:
> "....a man will leave his father and mother and unite with his wife, and the two will become one. So they are no longer two, but one. Man must not separate then, what God has joined together." Mark 10:7−9
>
> ▶ What do you think this means?

> From the Christian marriage ceremony:
> "With this ring I thee wed;
> With my body I thee honour and all my worldly goods with thee I share.
> In the name of the Father, the Son and the Holy Spirit."
>
> ▶ How is the ring (a circle) a symbol of marriage?

Work for your Folder

1 Write out this summary, filling in the gaps:

A Christian wedding takes place in ____. It is a joining of two people in the presence of ____. Christians see marriage as a lifelong ____. They believe that they should have only one partner. This is called ____. They also believe that ____ should be confined to marriage. Many Christians say that one purpose of marriage is to have ____.

children	church	monogamy
sex	commitment	God

2

B	O	U	Q	U	E	T	V
R	S	A	L	T	M	X	O
I	I	S	V	E	I	L	W
D	O	N	P	P	L	G	S
E	N	V	G	R	O	O	M
W	H	X	S	Y	V	D	B
C	F	K	J	B	E	L	L
C	H	U	R	C	H	S	T

Copy out and find *ten* words to do with a Christian marriage.

3 Draw the little cartoon couple on page 8. Suggest three captions for it which start "Marriage is...."

4 *I (name) do take thee (name) to be my lawful wedded wife/husband, to have and to hold from this day forward, for better, for worse, for richer, for poorer, in sickness and in health, to love and to cherish, till death do us part.*

This is the traditional wording of the marriage vows.
Some couples write their own vows.
What words would you like to use?
If you want the traditional wording, say why.
If you want new words—write them.

THINK AND DISCUSS

▶ Would you accept your parents' advice before starting a permanent relationship?

▶ What difference does it make when two people marry if they are both Christian believers?

▶ What difference does it make to the relationship a couple has if their religion prohibits sex before marriage?

ISSUE 3

Children — or not

A T.V. reporter asked six couples this question: "Did you discuss having children before you were married?"

Here are the replies:

Couple 1 "Yes, we said we wanted two children only. But we will wait about ten years. We *both* want a career."

Couple 2 "No. Now it is a problem. I want a baby. He doesn't."

Couple 3 "Why discuss it? The State only allows us to have two children."
(Couple from China)

Couple 4 "Of course. We both want as many children as God sends us."

Couple 5 "What is there to discuss? Surely everyone wants children. We are lucky that four of our children are still alive."
(Couple from El Salvador)

Couple 6 "Yes, and we think the world is over-populated. So we won't have our own children. Perhaps we will adopt a child."

TASK

Prepare a class debate. Here are some ideas to choose from.
- Contraception (artificial birth control) makes people selfish. Couples want pleasure without responsibility.
- If husband and wife share responsibilities and pleasure in child-raising, both can be fulfilled in their careers and home.
- Women should have babies not careers.
- The world is over-populated. Families should be limited.

Decide if you are *for* or *against* the statement. Prepare your argument for the next lesson.

A happy large family where each child is welcomed as God's gift

HELP! We can't have children

One in every ten couples discover they can't have children naturally.

Some possible solutions

Test-tube babies

The ovum (egg) is fertilized by male sperm *outside* the woman's body. The embryo is then put into her womb. A normal pregnancy continues. The ovum or sperm could be donated.

Surrogacy

This is womb-letting. A surrogate mother agrees to have a child for an infertile woman. Desperate couples have paid thousands of pounds for this. Paid surrogacy is now illegal in the U.K.

Fostering

Foster-parents look after a child for a period of time. The State pays something towards the child's keep. Some foster-parents have loved and cared for dozens of young people.

Adoption

This is a permanent arrangement (for life). Adoptive parents, by a legal agreement, become the substitute parents of a child. The responsibility is TOTAL.

There are very few babies for adoption in the U.K. Jackie and Joe went to South America for their children.

TASK

1 Match these half sentences and copy into your file.
1 One in every ten couples
2 Test-tube fertilization takes place
3 Another name for surrogacy
4 Foster-parents care for children
5 Adoption is a legal agreement

.... is "womb-letting".
.... over a period of time.
.... can't have children.
.... that is permanent.
.... outside the womb.

ISSUE 3 CHILDREN—OR NOT

What About Abortion?

Abortion is the ending of a pregnancy before birth.

In this photo (1988) people protest about M.P. David Alton's attempt to change the 1967 Abortion Act.

The Act says: an abortion may be performed up to the *28th week* of pregnancy IF
1 a mother's life is at risk,
2 her health is at risk,
3 another child would be an impossible burden,
4 there is risk of handicap for the baby.

The Pro-abortion Lobby say things like:
- The foetus is not yet a human life.
- It's a woman's right to choose.
- A handicapped child can be a burden.

The Anti-abortion Lobby say things like:
- A foetus is a human life. Abortion is murder.
- We are all handicapped in one way or another.
- Every human person is made in God's image.

TASK

Write to the following organizations for information:
- Abortion Law Reform Association, 88 Islington High Street, London N1 8EG.
- LIFE, 118–120 Warwick Street, Leamington Spa, Warwicks. CV32 4QY.
- Dr. Barnado's Homes, Barkingside, Essex 1G6 1QG.
- The Catholic Children's Society, 73 St. Charles Square, London W10 6EJ.

Display the material.

What do Christians Think?

	I AGREE	I DON'T AGREE
1 All Christians believe in the dignity of human life.		
2 They are very concerned about experiments made on embryos.		
3 Christians welcomed the condemnation of paid surrogacy.		
4 Many Christians are worried about the "test-tube" programme.		
5 The Roman Catholic Church condemns the test-tube programme.		
6 Orthodox and Protestant Christians may use artificial methods of birth-control (contraceptives).		
7 The Roman Catholic Church forbids the use of contraceptives.		
8 All Christians agree that abortion cannot be used to control birth.		
9 Some Christians allow abortion in the case of rape, or if the mother's life is in danger.		
10 The Roman Catholic Church forbids abortion totally.		

TASK

▶ Copy the above chart for your folder and complete the questionnaire by putting a tick in the appropriate column.

THE TABLET 27 June 1987

God had created us to love and to be loved, she said, in his own image, as evidence of his love. "For this reason I say that abortion is the greatest evil. If any one of you does not want his own child, do not kill it, but give it to me."
(This refers to Mother Theresa)

ISSUE 4

Prejudice

Young children, like Ben and Jaspreet, don't put up barriers between people. They simply accept all people as being of equal worth.

As we grow older we start making unfair judgements about others. This is called prejudice.

How does this happen?

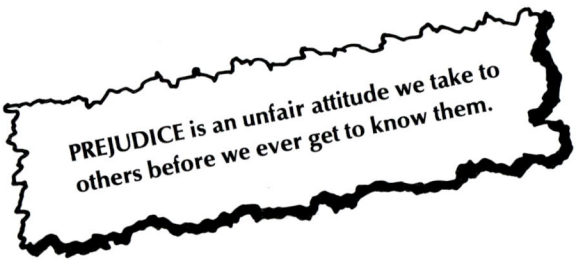

PREJUDICE is an unfair attitude we take to others before we ever get to know them.

TASK

1 ▶ This is where our prejudices can be formed and re-inforced:
ENVIRONMENT
TEACHING
PARENTS
FRIENDS
RELIGION
NEWSPAPERS
TELEVISION

Copy out and solve the puzzle.

1 Groups We all belong to a group. We show we belong by having "in" customs of behaviour and dress. Other people are kept outside of our group. We begin to feel better than the outsiders.

2 Fear We are afraid of things we don't know. The other groups seem to threaten us. We don't know what they think of us.

3 Scapegoats When things go wrong it is easy to blame someone else or another group. After the Hillsborough football disaster, the fans blamed the police. The police blamed the fans. (A scapegoat is someone *who carries the blame* for others.)

STEREOTYPES are the false or inaccurate pictures we build up in our minds of groups of people.

In describing groups of people it is difficult to avoid STEREOTYPES. I did not avoid them on pages 4, 25.

STEREOTYPES become unacceptable when we make judgements about groups we distrust or dislike.

Comments made when this man got off a bus.

1st Passenger: "What a sight! Young people today! They've got too much money to spend on themselves. I bet his crazy hair-style cost pounds."

2nd Passenger: "He'll be living off the State too. They never work. In fact they only think of themselves and what they can take from us."

Bus conductor: "They're so dirty. That's what I hate."

Heard on Derek Jameson's radio show
"I was in the middle of nowhere. My car spluttered to a halt. It was 1.30 am. I heard the roar of a motor bike overtake me. It stopped, turned and came back. My heart thumped when I saw the green-haired punk approach. "Run out of petrol," I shouted. He leapt on his bike and rode away. I was relieved. I thought he would mug me. Ten minutes later he returned with a can of petrol."

TASK

1 Here are two stereotype statements to do with the elderly:

"Old people never stop moaning."
"Old people always think they know best."

▶ Describe an elderly person you know who proves these stereotypes *wrong*.
2 Make a list of stereotype statements about young people, (e.g. "young people don't respect their elders").
▶ What stereotype statements about young people upset you most?
▶ Describe a friend who proves a stereotype *wrong*.

ISSUE 4 PREJUDICE

17

What do Christians Think?

Prejudice leads to discrimination. People are treated badly because of their; COLOUR, RACE, RELIGION, SEX.

Jesus treated *all* people as equal. The Christian Church has not always followed his example. In spite of this, there are many outstanding examples of Christians fighting *for* the rights of all people. Here are just a few examples:

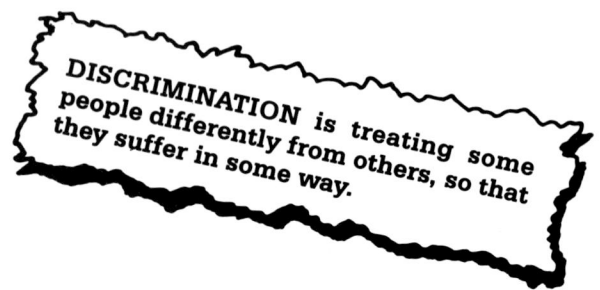
DISCRIMINATION is treating some people differently from others, so that they suffer in some way.

FAILURES	SUCCESSES
COLOUR South Africa's racial divide (apartheid) is the direct result of Christian Whites believing they are superior to Blacks.	Work of Martin Luther King, Trevor Huddleston, Archbishop Desmond Tutu, Rev. Allan Boesak.
RACE Christians have been guilty since the time of Jesus of persecuting the Jews (anti-semitism).	The Roman Catholic "Sisters of Sion" try to help Christians to respect and understand the Jews.
RELIGION Over centuries Christian groups have fought against each other, each group claiming to be "right".	A recent movement in the churches works towards unity (called ECUMENISM).
SEX The Christian Church, without realizing it, has always discriminated against women.	Slowly, women are speaking out in the Churches. There are a few women ministers today.

> ".... there is no difference between Jews and Gentiles, between slaves and free men, between men and women; you are all one in union with Christ Jesus."
> St. Paul to the Galatians 3:28

Work for your Folder

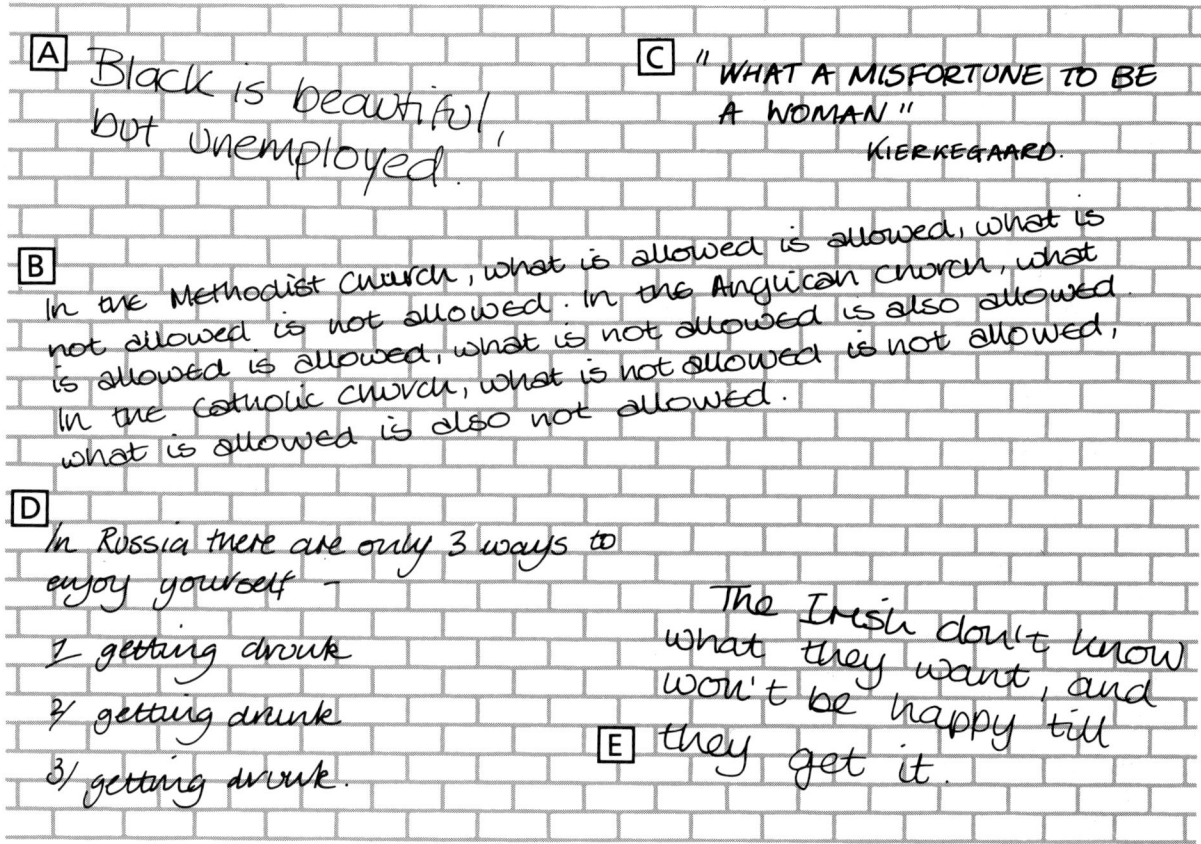

A: Black is beautiful, but unemployed.

B: In the Methodist Church, what is allowed is allowed, what is not allowed is not allowed. In the Anglican church, what is allowed is allowed, what is not allowed is also allowed. In the Catholic church, what is not allowed is not allowed, what is allowed is also not allowed.

C: "WHAT A MISFORTUNE TO BE A WOMAN" KIERKEGAARD.

D: In Russia there are only 3 ways to enjoy yourself —
1/ getting drunk
2/ getting drunk
3/ getting drunk.

E: The Irish don't know what they want, and won't be happy till they get it.

1 Write out definitions for Prejudice, Stereotypes, Discrimination.

2 Four school-leavers apply for the same job. The three who did not get the job claimed discrimination (each for a different reason).
   a Describe the job.
   b Describe the successful applicant.
   c Make up three letters of complaint from the unsuccessful applicants.

3 Look at the wall of graffiti above. Graffiti often show prejudice or discrimination.

a Which of the four types of discrimination (page 18) are represented by each piece of graffiti?
b Describe a person who is likely to have written graffito A.
c Read carefully graffito B. In what way are the three church denominations made into stereotypes?
b In what way are Irish jokes stereotypes?
e Think carefully if you have any prejudices. (Look at the four types on page 18.) Do you think anyone is prejudiced against you? Discuss these questions in your group.

ISSUE 5

Handicap

This group of High School pupils decided to do more than talk about "handicap" in class.

They got together and organized dinner-time activities.

They raised over £50 in one week for physically handicapped children.

TASK

People suffer from many physical handicaps.

1 Make a list of the physical handicaps you know about.

2 Imagine you have £100 to give to a society that works for handicapped people. Which group would you support?

3 Draw a class graph or chart to compare your choices.

4 Do what this class did and plan some fund-raising events in your school.

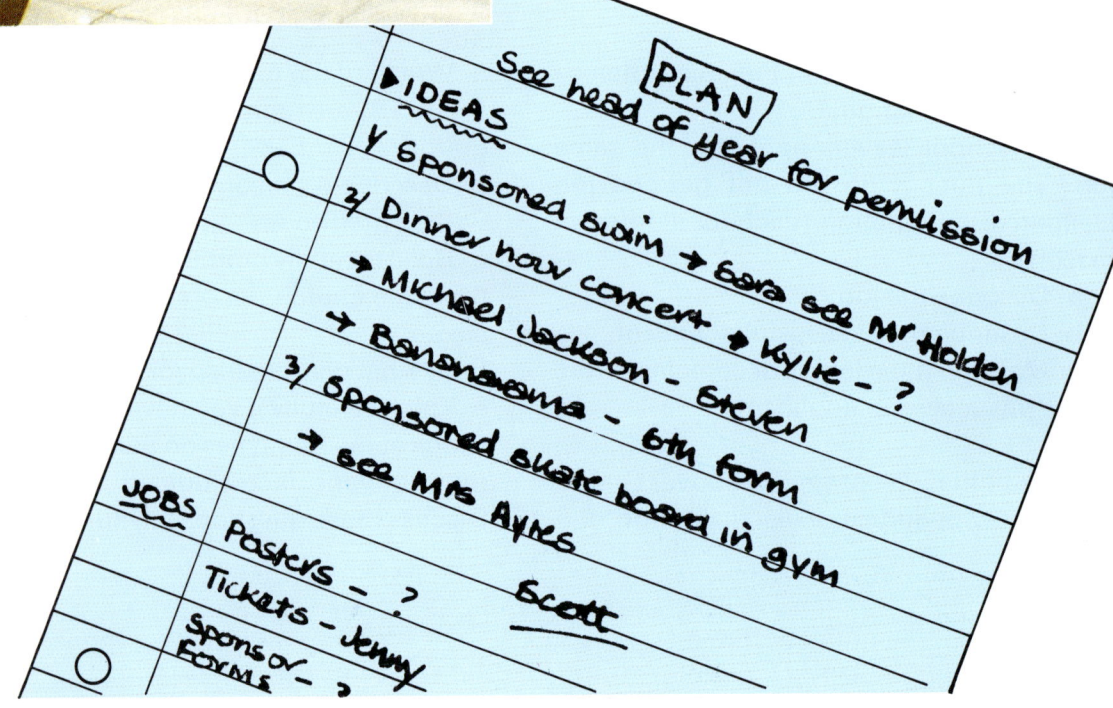

L'Arche

In **L'Arche Communities** family life and daily work are fully shared with people who have mental handicaps.

▶ *Who founded L'Arche?*
The Communities were the idea of JEAN VANIER, a French-Canadian. He formed his first community in France, in 1964.

Today there are over 60 communities world-wide.

▶ *Who are the Members of L'Arche?*
1 The handicapped people. They are the heart of the community.
2 The assistants who share their life. Many are young people from different back-grounds. Some come for a year or so, others have decided to make L'Arche their home.

▶ *What about professional help?*
The communities are helped by professional medical staff and by people with useful work skills.

▶ *What is special about L'Arche?*
The L'Arche Communities are based on the ideals of the Christian Gospel (Bible).
- Everyone shares what he or she has.
- Everyone works and prays together.

TASK

1 In the Bible find Acts of the Apostles, Chapter 2, Verses 44–47.
In what way is a L'Arche Community similar to the first Christian community described here?

TASK G

Write to a L'Arche Community in England or Scotland and ask for more information.

Kent,
"Little Ewell",
Barfrestone,
Nr. Dover,
Kent CT15 7JJ
(0304) 830930

Inverness,
"Braerannoch",
13 Drummond Crescent,
Inverness IV2 4HD
Scotland
(0463) 239615

Liverpool,
"The Bridge",
127 Prescot Road,
Liverpool 6
(051) 260 0422

"Lambeth",
1 Dunbar Street,
West Norwood,
London SE27
(01) 670 6714
(01) 761 4860

Bognor Regis,
"Sea Rover",
4 Argyle Circus,
Bognor Regis,
West Sussex
(0243) 863426

What do Christians Think?

Christians are not the only ones who work for or with handicapped people. But the Gospel (Christian Bible) is full of stories where Jesus cured people who suffered physically or mentally.

This has inspired some Christians to work alongside handicapped people.

"The child who is physically, mentally or socially handicapped shall be given the special treatment, education and care required by his particular condition."
United Nations Declaration.

JEAN VANIER is a Christian. He wrote: "Living daily with mentally handicapped people I have discovered in them a world of goodness. Qualities, often hidden deep in their hearts, can only develop when they feel secure and live in an atmosphere of work, peace and joy . . . and when they are respected."

LEONARD CHESHIRE is also a Christian. His whole life is spent caring for physically handicapped people. There are 75 Cheshire Homes in the U.K. As a bomber pilot in World War II he saw the atomic bomb released over Nagasaki. This horror changed his life.

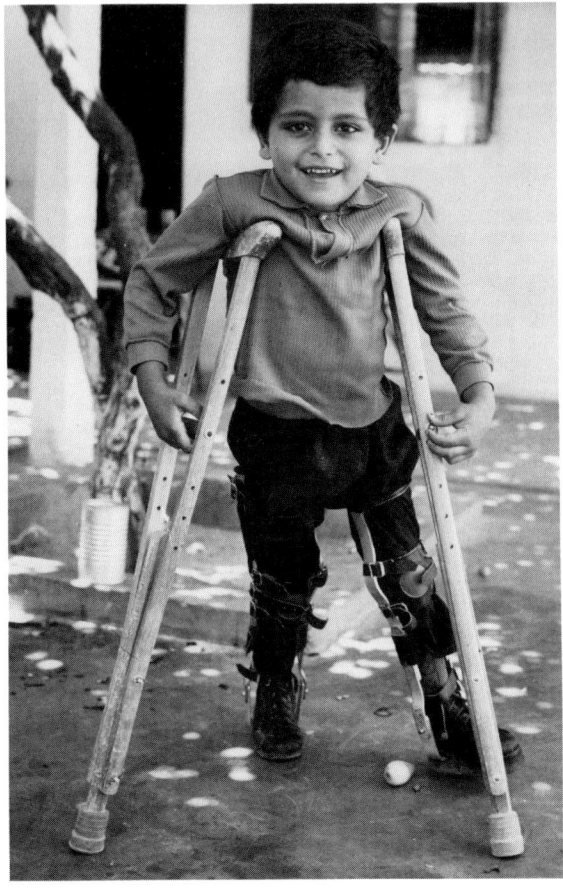

THINK ABOUT IT AND DISCUSS

▶ How would you cope with a severe handicap like the boy in the photo?
▶ How would you want to be treated?
▶ An advert for the Spastics Society says: "Our biggest handicap is other people's attitude."
What does this mean?

Work for your Folder

1 John broke his leg in a car crash. He will be in a wheelchair for months. Can he come to school?

   a Get a plan of your school (or draw one).

   b Make a list of all the subjects taught in your school.

   c Draw and fill in a chart like the one below:

SUBJECT	ROOMS USED
English	all on ground floor
CDT	in mobile (with steps)
Maths	in ....

   d How is John going to get to classes? Work out what changes would need to be made for John to attend classes.

2 Do you know these logos? Match them with the list of organizations below.

Phab
Mencap
L'Arche

Design your own logo for the Great Ormond Street Hospital in London.

3 Look through Luke's Gospel and list some stories which tell of Jesus curing people.

Choose one story and retell it as though you are the cured person.

ISSUE 6

Pain, Old Age and Death

Pain

Luke, one of the Gospel writers, was a doctor. He was impressed by Jesus' power of healing. His Gospel speaks of Jesus as a compassionate man, who wanted to take away pain and suffering from people.

Christians have always believed that they must try to do the same.

TASK

I Some Christians work to relieve suffering. At the same time they look at Jesus' suffering on a cross as their way of salvation.

List some ways in which you think suffering can be used for good.

G Discuss your list with people in your group.

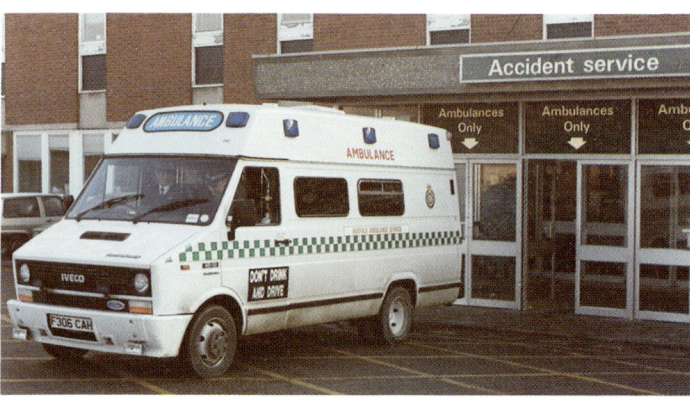

Christian monks founded the first hospitals. Many existing hospitals were built by Christians in the 18th century.

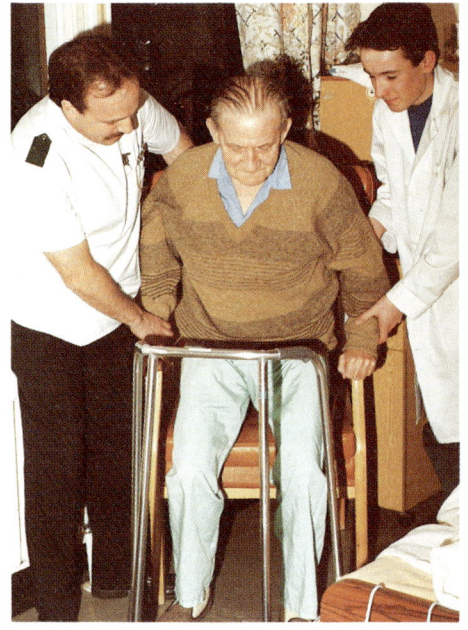

Many Christians choose nursing as a profession

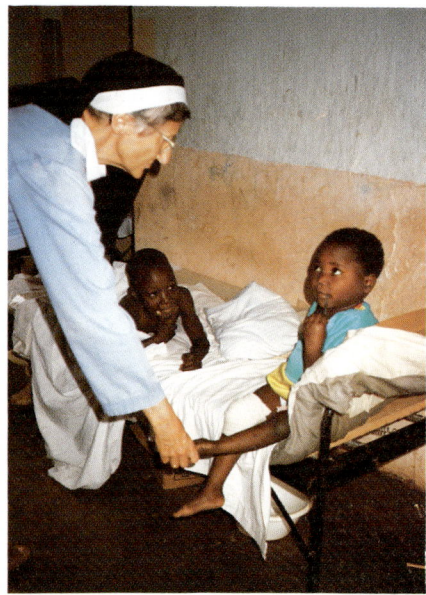

Christian missionaries go all over the world to nurse, and relieve suffering

St. John's Ambulance Brigade was founded in 1099 in Jerusalem, during the Crusades

Old Age

People today live longer than they used to. How do elderly and retired people keep active and contented? Not all of them do. Compare Enid with Ron.

Enid:

lives with daughter and family, loves knitting for them, baby-sits for her grandchildren, is included in family decisions, but has her *own* life and privacy.

Ron:

lives alone in a new bungalow, his family rarely visit, he feels useless and a burden, he worries about money, he doesn't like having his meals at a day-centre.

TASK

What would you want in your old age?

	A Very important	B Important	C Less important
Good health			
Family visits			
Own home			
Friends			
Garden			
Good food			
Some work			
Leisure activities			
Good heating system			
Religious beliefs			
Good sight			
Good hearing			
Telephone			
Wealth			
Holidays			
A home help			

Copy out this table and fill in.
Compare your results with others.
Make a display of the joint results.

TASK

Enid and Ron are rather stereotyped.

Describe an elderly person who does not share their experience.

TASK

▶ Invite local workers from these two organizations to visit your school/group.

TASK

▶ Interview your grandmother or grandfather or an elderly neighbour. Use a tape recorder.

Death

> *Reflection*
> Those who love in the Lord never see each other for the last time.

Most Christians believe that death is not the end. It is the gateway to a new life in PARADISE (heaven).

For Christians this belief is based on the death and resurrection of Jesus. They believe that the sadness of their death will lead to joy, as it did for Jesus.

Life after death remains a MYSTERY. But Christians remain convinced that the dead are with God, because they are loved by God.

Dying can be painful both for those who die and for those who are bereaved. But it need not be. Two outstanding Christian women have been concerned to show that the last days of a person's life are as important as the first days.

Dame Cecily Saunders
founded the *Hospice Movement* to provide special homes for the dying, where:
pain is controlled,
families are welcomed,
patients are prepared for death,
the atmosphere is relaxed, even joyful.

Mother Teresa
has founded homes all over the world, beginning among the poorest of the poor in Calcutta. She is convinced that the very poor should die with love and respect. Her Christian belief is that life NOW is as important as "after-life".

> "... Death is destroyed; victory is complete!
> Where Death, is your victory?
> Where Death, is your power to hurt? ....
> Thanks be to God who gives us the victory through our Lord Jesus Christ!"
> 1 Corinthians 15 : 54–57

Work for your Folder

1 *Copy this for your folder, filling in the missing words:*

The Gospel writer Luke, was a ____. He showed that ____ was a compassionate man who took away people's pain. Christians ____ that they should do the same. The first ____ were founded by monks. Many Christians choose to be nurses, and some go as ____ to help the sick in other lands. St. John's Ambulance Brigade was founded in ____, in the 11th century, to nurse wounded Christian crusaders.

| missionaries | doctor | hospitals |
| Jerusalem | believe | Jesus |

2 a Make a list of the things you might *fear* most in old age.
b In your group compare your lists. Make a single list of all your fears.
c From the "group list" choose the FIVE things that are most feared, in order of importance.
d Different groups compare results. Show these results on the notice-board.

3 *Word search*

a Copy out this word-search grid.
b Copy the text below into your files. Find the underlined words in the grid.

The Mystery of Death

Christians believe that death is not the end. It is the beginning of life in heaven. Life after death is a mystery. But Christians believe that the dead are held in the real love of God. Two women who work with the dying are Mother Teresa and Cecily Saunders.

Mother Teresa's first home for the dying was in India. She said that the poor could at least die knowing love and respect.

Cecily Saunders founded Hospices in this country. In these homes the dying are prepared for death. Their pain is controlled. Families are made welcome. The hospices are so relaxed and caring that the sorrow of death is even turned to joy. This joy comes from faith in God.

M	O	T	H	E	R	T	E	R	E	S	A	X
Y	R	J	O	Y	X	E	M	O	C	L	E	W
S	E	Y	S	A	U	N	D	E	R	S	H	H
T	S	W	P	E	I	D	Y	S	D	N	E	O
E	P	O	I	A	P	A	I	N	D	I	A	M
R	E	M	C	N	O	T	N	O	L	O	V	E
Y	C	E	E	P	O	L	G	L	I	F	E	K
K	T	N	S	O	R	R	O	W	O	H	N	A
O	F	M	D	E	A	T	H	H	T	I	A	F

ISSUE 6 PAIN, OLD AGE AND DEATH

ISSUE 7
Housing and Healing the World

Introduction

A Christian called Irenaeus, who lived in the 3rd century AD said, "God comes alive in a person who is fully human."

Some people argue that those who live in great poverty, sickness and misery cannot live fully human lives. So there are Christian groups and individuals who work to remove injustice.

There are four main areas of need:

- **HOUSING**
- **HEALING**
- **FEEDING**
- **EDUCATING**

Here is how some Christians in Norwich are helping to house people in need.

SISTER PAMELA is an Anglican nun. She shares her home with homeless women. They go to her, at Little Portion Mission House, when they are desperate. The police, social workers, Samaritans or the NSPCC send women and children to her. They stay long enough to sort out their lives. When they move on, Sr. Pamela often helps them to set up their new homes.

The Catholic Parish of St. John's, in Norwich, has adopted a parish in Peru. Every week the parishioners collect, on average, £60 to send to the Notre Dame Sisters in Tambogrande. (There is a Notre Dame school in Norwich.) A few years ago *all* the houses were destroyed in floods. The Norwich parish sent enough money to buy *every* family in Tambogrande new corrugated iron roofing.

TASKS

1 Some people would say that it is the wealthy who do not live fully human lives. Explain what you think they mean by this.

2 There are probably homeless people in your town.
Can you give reasons for this?
Can you offer a solution?

HEALING

Compare these two cases:

A Peter, age 20, had his foot crushed in an accident in a farm-machine. His foot is being rebuilt. He will be in hospital for months. *COST:* £8,000.

B Pedro, age 2, is a farmer's son in Bolivia. He had gastroenteritis (severe stomach trouble). He died from dehydration (i.e. he needed liquid). *COST* of medicine which would have saved him: 30 p.

Many Christians are concerned about how unequal medical care can be. Some go out to Third World countries to nurse people like Pedro.

Mary Martin was born in Ireland years ago. She had bad health all her life. It made her want to help other sick people. In 1936 she founded a religious congregation. This means that other young women joined her and went to nurse the sick in Africa. Her congregation is called MEDICAL MISSIONARIES of Mary. Mother Mary Martin died in 1975, but her work continues. Today the sisters work as nurses, doctors, social workers or pharmacists in Africa and South America. Most of the sisters train for medical work at a hospital built by Mother Mary Martin in Drogheda, Ireland. It is called the International Training Hospital.

TASK

1. Copy out and solve the crossword.
Note: all answers are in the previous passage.

Clues across

1 Surname of Mother Mary.
2 A continent where the sisters work today (two words).
3 Mother Mary's country of birth.
4 Many of her sisters train to be ____.
5 This lady's first name.
6 The training hospital is in this town.

Clues down

1 A Christian who goes to work in other countries.
7 The sisters train for this kind of work.
8 The continent where Mother Mary first worked.

What do Christians Think?

Christians believe that since God loves and cares for each person, they must do the same.

CHRISTIAN AID and CAFOD are two organizations which try to do this by helping the world's poor:
1 by immediate practical help,
2 by trying to deal with the CAUSE of poverty.

CHRISTIAN AID is the largest Christian organization to help the world's poor. It is part of the British Council of Churches. This means it is supported by many Christian churches.

Every year Christian Aid raises over £10 million to help the poorest of the poor in the world to help themselves. Here at home it helps people understand what causes such poverty.

CAFOD means Catholic Fund for Overseas Development. It was set up by Roman Catholic Bishops in England and Wales in 1962. Every year there is a Family Fast Day. Families go hungry and send the money they save to help CAFOD projects.

Today CAFOD helps over 500 communities in 75 countries. Like Christian Aid, CAFOD helps people to help themselves.

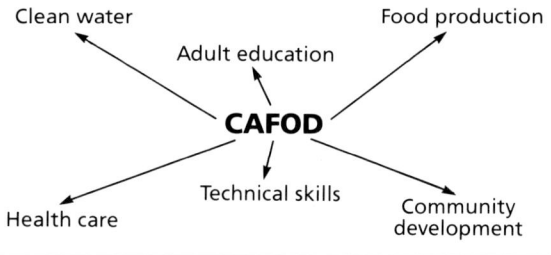

TASKS

1 Every May there is a *Christian Aid Week* to raise funds.

Design a poster to display in your school entrance hall.

OR

2 CAFOD has a programme *"Working in Partnership"*, linking schools and parishes here with overseas projects.

Design a poster to show your school linked with a school overseas.

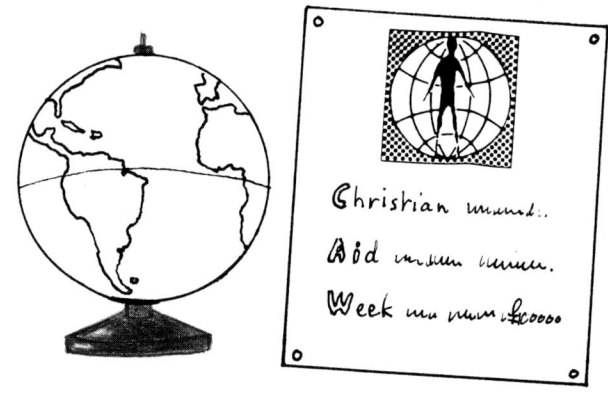

Work for your Folder

1. > John, aged 61, needs a heart by-pass operation.
    > Sandra, aged 31, mother of two, needs a new kidney.
    > Sarah, aged 10, needs a bone-marrow transplant.
    > All three will die without immediate surgery. But there is only enough money in the NHS to treat ONE.

Work in threes.
One will speak on behalf of John.
One will speak for Sandra.
One will speak for Sarah.
Argue *your* case for having the operation.

2 Write to the following organizations for information:
SHELTER
157 Waterloo Rd., London SE1 8UU.
6 Castle Street, Edinburgh EH2 3AT.
CYRENIANS
13 Wincheap, Canterbury, Kent CT1 3TB.
SAMARITANS
17 Uxbridge Road, Slough SL1 1SN.
MEDICAL MISSIONARIES OF MARY
2 Denbigh Road, Ealing W13 8PX.

▶ When you get some information make decorated information sheets to encourage the public to support the organization.
▶ Display all your information sheets.

3 Divide up into four groups. Each group takes one of the four areas of need described on page 28
   Housing   Healing
   Feeding   Education

▶ Each group prepares a collage for the notice-board. (Use newspaper cuttings, magazines etc.)
▶ Show the contrast between our country and the Third World.

ISSUE 8

Feeding and Educating the World

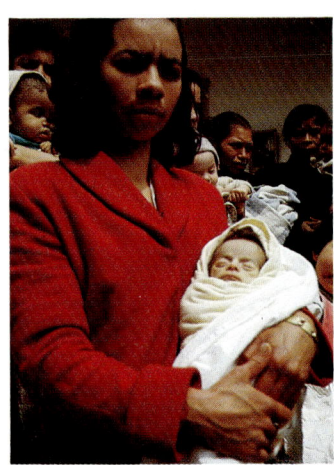

Feeding the Body

Two-thirds of the world go to bed hungry. Every day thousands of children die of hunger. Most of the world's poor and hungry people live in the

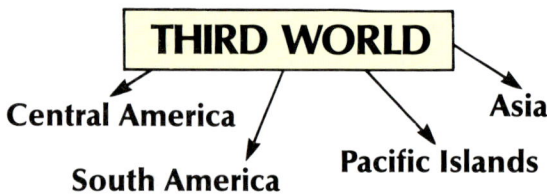

> A politician once said that television would enable us to sit at home and watch each other starve.

We live in the rich one-third of the world. Most of us can fill up a supermarket trolley of food each week. Many people need to go on diets because *we eat too much*. We are in the

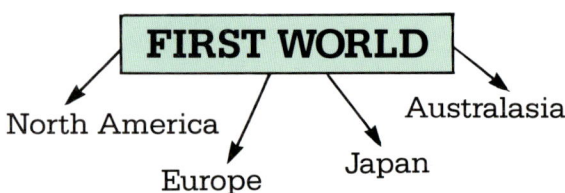

But the world is ONE WORLD. What we do in the U.K. affects people in the rest of the world. Take one example:

The Supermarket Age

92% of supermarket food is pre-packed. This is costly. The losers are:

1 the environment (trees cut down for paper and packing),
2 energy supplies (which are rapidly used up—especially oil),
3 our health (through too many additives),
4 small farmers and communities (who are put out of work).

TASK

▶ Imagine that your class has been asked to lead an assembly for ONE-WORLD WEEK.
▶ Make a set of posters using words from this page, with magazine cut-outs.
OR
▶ In groups work out a way to present the information on this page on the stage as a play or mime.

What do Christians Think?

Many Christians see a direct relationship between feeding the hungry and the community celebration of the Eucharist or Communion.

A Methodist broadcaster, Pauline Webb, visited a village in Chile. A poor man offered her a piece of bread. He said, in broken English, "Take, eat." These are the words used by Christians when they receive bread as the "Body of Christ" in their Eucharist celebration. Pauline said that eating bread with the man *was* a kind of Eucharist.

Christians inherited from the Jews an understanding of God's concern for the hungry.

"His disciples asked him, 'where in this desert can anyone find enough food to feed all those people?'"   Mark 8:4

"Every third year give a tenth of your crops to the Levites, the foreigners, the orphans and the widows, so that in every community they will have all they need to eat."
Deuteronomy 26:12

Most Christians are likely to support campaigns to feed the world.

"I'm not interested in the bloody system! Why is he starving to death?"   Bob Geldof

Work for your Folder

1 Take two sheets of file paper. Head one *THIRD WORLD* and the other *FIRST WORLD*.
▶ Copy out information from these pages on to your two sheets.
▶ Find a newspaper advert/cutting for each sheet (e.g. diet plan and Oxfam advert).

2

We spend more on bedtime hot drinks than we do on giving aid to the Third World.

▶ Use this information to make a collection envelope for a ONE-WORLD WEEK campaign.

ISSUE 8 FEEDING AND EDUCATING THE WORLD

Feeding the Mind (Education)

Millions of children in the Third World don't go to school. They are starved of education.

Read this question to Christian Aid (a charity which helps Third World countries).

> **Q.** It is very hard to get my church to support Christian Aid, when I talked to my minister about it last week he said he thought feeding people's minds was more important than feeding their bodies.
>
> **A.** We tend to think of feeding bodies and feeding minds as two very different things. But God created people as whole human beings. Bodies and minds cannot be completely separated.
> Christian Aid does not simply feed people's bodies. We are concerned about them as people. We believe that God does not want people to go hungry or to suffer injustice. If Christians are not helping the poor there is something seriously wrong.

1 What do you think is more important, to feed hungry people, or to feed people's minds (educate)?
Give reasons for your choice.

2 The answer says that there is something wrong if Christians are not helping the poor. Can you give a reason for this statement?

Compare pictures A and B

A

Photo A Children at an English First School learn through play.
They have TIME to learn—at least 10 years of education lie ahead of them.

B

Photo B These boys will be lucky to have 3 or 4 years of education.
Their school is a hut with a blackboard. They have one book and one slate.

TASK

Make a list of all the equipment (large and small)
1 you used at your primary school,
2 you use in this school.
3 Look at the boy in photo B. His list will have only three items: blackboard, books and slate.
What is your *immediate* reaction?
a That's hard luck, but not my problem.
b Something must be done to make it more equal.
Compare your reply with others in your group. Explain your replies.

What do Christians Think?

The Christian Church in the past took a leading role in education in Europe. It still does in the Third World. Christians believe that feeding the mind is as important as feeding the body.

Four examples of Christian concern for education

- In the Middle Ages monks taught reading and writing and later set up universities.
- In the 16th century the Church founded many of our famous public schools.
- In the 18th–19th century religious orders were founded to educate the poor.
- The development of industry in the 19th century brought with it great poverty. Christians like Lord Shaftesbury, introduced laws to improve life for children in Britain. Christians set up Poor Schools.

This nun is a member of a Roman Catholic religious order which was founded 150 years ago, to educate the poor.

Sister Claudia is in an Andean village in Colombia. This new school was built with help from Catholic schools in Germany.

Work for your Folder

▶ Copy out and find the ten listed words in the Wordsearch Square below.
▶ Write a summary of these four pages. You must include the *ten* words in your summary.
▶ Underline the ten words.

THINK ABOUT IT

Think BIG. Why not get your school to "twin" with a Third-World school?

| EDUCATION |
| HUNGER |
| SCHOOL |
| GELDOF |
| EUCHARIST |
| DIET |
| EUROPE |
| NUNS |
| TROLLEY |
| MONKS |

S	H	E	M	P	D	X	T	F
E	D	U	C	A	T	I	O	N
U	Y	C	L	M	Z	K	E	S
R	E	H	U	N	G	E	R	T
O	L	A	P	U	E	R	V	S
P	L	R	B	N	L	C	K	D
E	O	I	S	S	D	N	F	G
J	R	S	C	H	O	O	L	O
Q	T	T	V	M	F	W	T	H

ISSUE 9

Work and Unemployment

Work

We meet someone for the first time. One of the first questions we are likely to ask is: "What do you do?" Some people dread the question because they are unemployed.

Work is important because it meets many of our basic needs.
1 It makes us part of the adult world.
2 It allows us to meet other people.
3 It gives us a place in society.
4 It gives us a purpose in life.
5 It gives us responsibility.
6 It provides us with money.
7 It enables us to help others.

TASK

I ▶ Look carefully at the seven reasons given here why work is important.
▶ Write them out in the order YOU think is most important to you.

Work in Britain

● In our society work is controlled by laws that have been developed over the years.
● These laws safeguard the rights of workers (employees).
● We owe this to TRADE UNIONS, a movement which was developed to protect workers from greedy and unjust employers.

Work in many Third World countries

● But millions of people have no Trade Unions to insist on fair wages and safe working conditions.
● The three areas of greatest concern are:
1 *Cheap labour:* "Boys work in a cyanide pool at a gold mine and earn 50p for an 8-hour shift."

2 *Exploitation of women workers:* "These African women work 17 hours a day, ten in the fields, the rest as wives and mothers." (See photo above.)

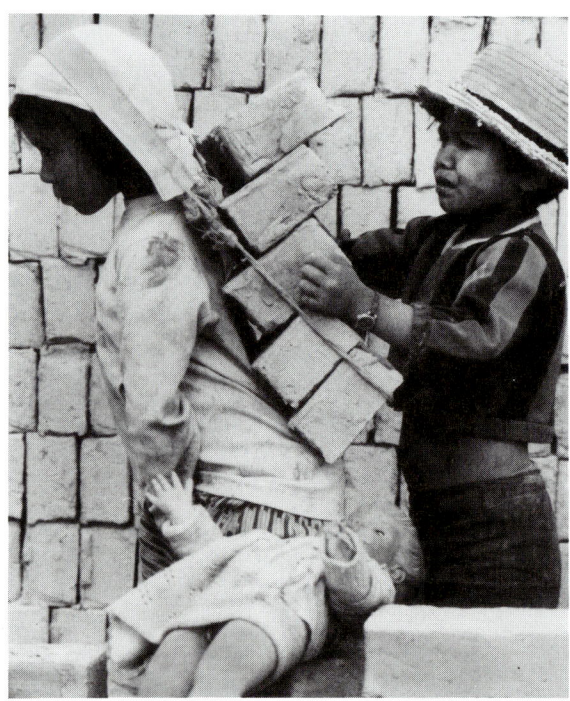

3 *Child labour:* "Children of 6 years old work in South America." (See photo above.)

Unemployment

The work scene in the U.K. is changing:

18-19th century
Farming

19-20th century
Industry

20th-21st century
Technology

The change from the age of industry to the age of technology is causing massive unemployment problems today.

1 Problems of the individual

"I feel depressed. I can't give my family a decent life."

"I'm bored stiff. I just stay in bed most of the day now."

"No one is going to employ me now. I'm 51."

"I can't feed the children, pay the rent *and* buy new shoes."

"What's the point of living? I'm useless now."

"I hate living on charity."

2 Problems for the community

"I can't stand living in this town. It's rundown. No one will buy my house."

"There are no young people here anymore. They've left to find work elsewhere."

"We see our husbands once a month. They've gone to work in London."

"What's the point of working for exams? I'll not get a job when I leave school."

TASKS

1 Think of ways an individual can use a period of unemployment to his/her own benefit.

2 Think of ways an individual can use a period of unemployment for the benefit of the community.

3 Design an attractive poster to advertise one of your ideas.

What do Christians Think?

Christians have different attitudes towards work. Perhaps this is because the Bible takes different attitudes at different times.

Six people were asked about their work. Here are their replies.

A I've chosen to be a nurse because I want to help people.
B I only ever look forward to my weekends off.
C I don't worry about getting a job. Things always work out.
D I have to work to keep my family clothed and fed.
E Work isn't the only thing in life, you know!
F I work very hard. The results are worth it.

Here are six Bible texts. Look them up.

TEXT	MAIN IDEA
Genesis 2:3	God set aside the seventh day to rest after completing his work.
Proverbs 19:15	Be lazy if you want to but you will go hungry.
Ephesians 6:5–8	God rewards the good worker.
Matthew 6:26–29	God looks after birds and flowers without them having to work.
Mark 10:43	Work should be a service to others.
Luke 10:38–42	Work is not always the most important thing.

TASK

Can you match the six replies **A–F** with the six texts? Example: **A** → Mark 10:43
The six replies show different attitudes towards work.

Discuss them in your group.
Are some attitudes more worthwhile than others? Why?

Increasing unemployment could have one positive result. It could lead to the collapse of an old Christian idea that work is a sacred duty—*the* way to heaven. This view makes unemployed people feel guilty. Most Christians today value people for who they are, not for what they do.

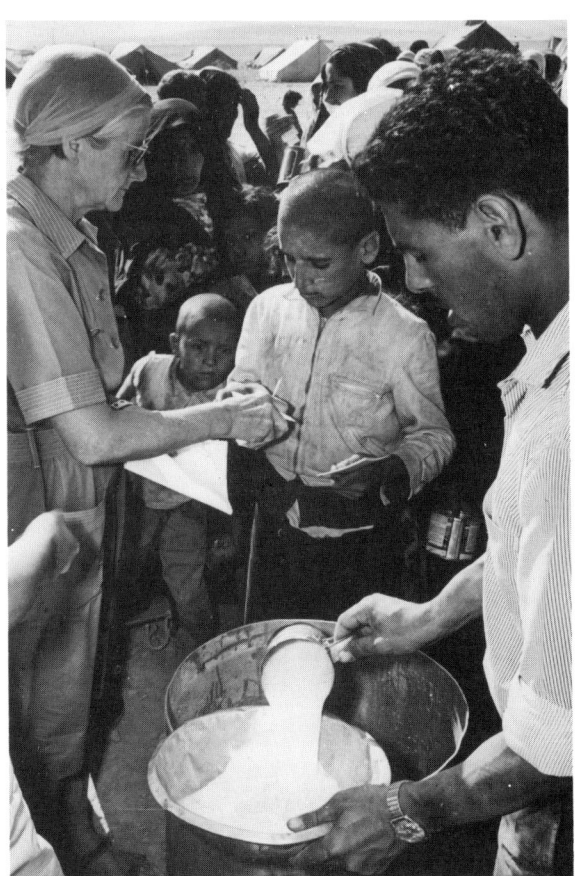

Work should be a service to others

Work for your Folder

1

> **Doesn't want to work**
>
> My 20-year-old son has been unemployed since he left school two years ago with excellent A levels. He shows no desire to work and appears to be happy doing nothing very much.
> He sleeps late, spends winter in the library reading and the summer sunbathing by the sea. He has plenty of friends, few expenses and fits in very well at home. But I worry about his future and my friends look at me oddly when I talk about him. Incidentally he doesn't live off the State. He does odd-job gardening and manages on that.

▶ Write a reply to "Worried Mother".

2 Copy out this chart and tick the appropriate columns.
▶ Get into groups to compare answers.
▶ Make a graph or bar chart to show the results.

Would you?	Yes	No	Don't know
1 Work in a factory making parts for nuclear bombs?			
2 Work on low pay in order to help the Third World?			
3 Take a day off work and make up an excuse?			
4 Pocket a few spare parts from the garage you work in?			
5 Work on Sundays?			
6 Strike for more pay even though it puts others out of work?			
7 Accept a pay cut to help others?			
8 Listen to parents' wishes about a career?			
9 Accept a dangerous job for the challenge?			
10 Change your shift at short notice to help others out?			
11 Lie about your age to get a Saturday job?			
12 Moonlight (take on a second job unlawfully—usually at night)?			
13 Give up your job in order to care for a sick relative?			
14 Do volunteer work overseas?			
15 Work for a tobacco company?			
16 Do research work on embryos?			
17 If you are a woman would you return to work immediately after the birth of a baby?			
18 Notify your employer of a wage mistake in your favour?			
19 Take part in a job-sharing scheme?			
20 Leave your job if you thought your employer was immoral?			

ISSUE 10

Leisure

This is how a dictionary defines "leisure". But it *feels* different to each person. Here are 5 people and their 5 comments on leisure. Match the person with the comment.

lei'sure n. free time, time at one's own disposal;

Comments
"Leisure, when do I have time for that?"
"Leisure? It's every moment I'm not in my job."
"I've too much leisure. I hate it—I can't fill the hours."
"Leisure is squash, jogging and a round of golf."
"What's leisure? I sit for hours waiting for news of my husband."

People
Low-paid factory worker
Young bank manager
Mother of 5 young children
Wife of Lebanese soldier
Unemployed man

TASK

1. Compare these children:

A

B

Photo A Stephen's father manages a youth football team. Stephen promises to be a star player. The family's Saturday revolves around playing and watching football (they support Spurs).

Photo B This girl in a shanty town has plenty of free time but not many facilities on the hillside.
▶ Write a page of Stephen's Dad's diary. Date: Saturday, Oct. 5th.
▶ Write a page of young Lucia's diary. Same date.

It has always been recognized that people need relaxation from work—(including a break from school study). It is more than "filling in time".

Leisure is good because:
1 We need rest.
2 We need active recreation.
3 We need the chance to develop our talents (skills).
4 We need social contacts (meeting other people).

Today, leisure is becoming an *industry*. This means there are more opportunities for those who can pay.

Sports Villages, Leisure Centres and Pleasure Parks are being built everywhere. Drama and music workshops are set up for young people. Not everyone can afford to go to them.

TASKS

1 List as many leisure activities as you can.
▶ Sort them out. Copy into your folder under the four "needs" above.
Example: *We need rest* Watching T.V.
                                    Knitting....

2 Interview your class/year group.
Record two leisure activities per person.
▶ Display the results in a colourful way.

What do Christians Think?

Christians see rest and enjoyment as part of God's plan. In the Jewish/Christian creation story God himself rests on the seventh day:

> "He blessed the seventh day and set it apart as a special day...." Genesis 2:3

In another Old Testament text, God is seen as encouraging people to take time away from work:

> "You have six days in which to do your work, but the seventh day is a day of rest dedicated to me. On that day no one is to work...." Exodus 20:9–10

Jesus, the busy preacher, and his disciples needed rest. Mark wrote:

> "....Jesus and his disciples didn't even have time to eat. So he said... 'Let us go off by ourselves.... and you can rest for a while.'" Mark 6:31

In the past Christians used Sunday rest from work as time for going to church and reading the Bible. Even housework was frowned on. Most Christians today use Sunday rest as

time for worship,
time for family,
time for oneself,
time for leisure.

TASKS

1 ▶ Make a list of ten ways you can use leisure time to help other people.

▶ Check with people whether your ideas are good ones.

▶ Why not try them out?

A day of rest "dedicated to God"?

Work for your Folder

1 Draw a plan of a community and leisure centre, showing different things it caters for. It is being built in a part of the town which has:
a a housing estate full of young families,
b a large hospital/home for handicapped people.

2 Draw a cartoon which has the caption: "All work and no play makes Jack a dull boy."

3 Read the Genesis story of creation. (Genesis 1:1–2:4.)
▶ Design a picture or collage of this creation story.
▶ Make the seventh day of rest the most important part of the picture.

4 A mathematical exercise:
work out (roughly) the cost of taking part in leisure activities.
Present your results in a chart which will look something like this:

FOR DISCUSSION

1 In future people will work fewer hours and have more leisure time. But will they be able to afford leisure activities?
2 Are some leisure pursuits better than others? Why?

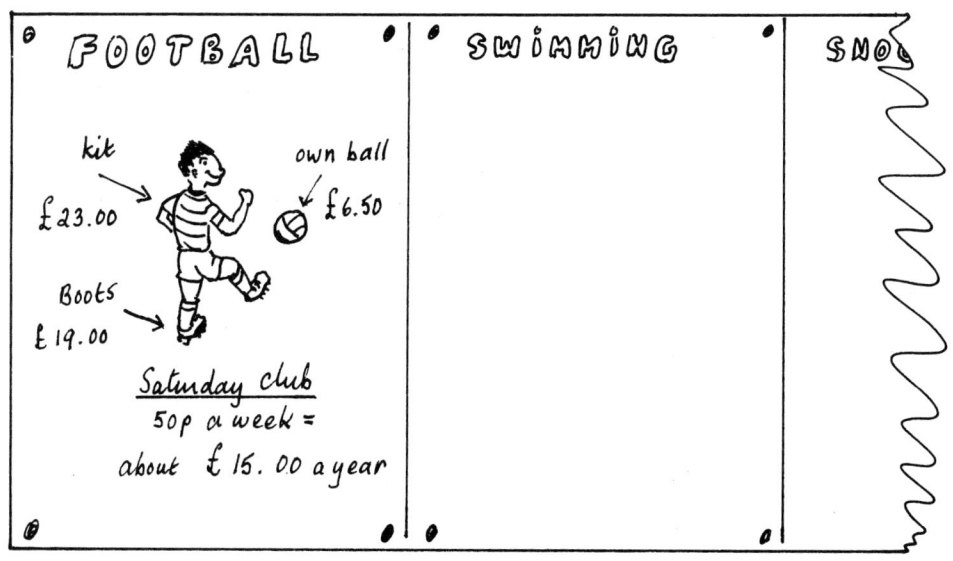

Money and Possessions

ISSUE 11

Some Christians living in the Western World feel in a dilemma. They are part of a world economic system which keeps them comfortable at the expense of millions of people living in poverty. This is against everything Jesus stood for.

THE WAGE OR SALARY In the U.K. most people earn a wage or salary by working. Part of this wage goes to the government as "tax". Part of this tax provides "security" for the unemployed, so that their 4 basic needs are met:
food, housing, clothing, heating

CAPITALISM Individuals have CAPITAL—money which they can exchange for goods, and can use to increase their own wealth.

Some Christians are now criticizing this system, because it makes rich people get richer and the poor stay poor.

INVESTMENT Today many people put money into a business project and share in the profits.

SOCIALISM was influenced in its beginnings by Christians who wanted the community, not individuals, to own and control trade.

BORROWING Many people borrow money from banks or building societies. The money must be paid back with INTEREST ("fee" for service).

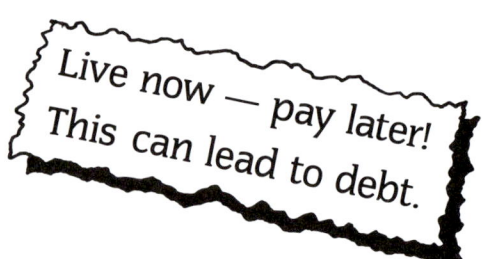

Live now — pay later! This can lead to debt.

Two-thirds of the world's population struggle to survive. Both photos on this page illustrate this struggle.

Debt is a terrible burden. This South American country has borrowed heavily from the West. It finds it difficult to pay the debt.

Brazil has had to set up a number of land schemes to make money to pay off its debts. This means its people stay unfed. Christians are amongst those in the West who are beginning to press their Governments to cancel all Third World debt.

These South African Blacks are forced to work away from their families. They spend only one day a month at home. The system turns members of the black community into second-class citizens.

In the U.K. today some families are undergoing the same experience. Many men have to leave home to find jobs, and can only return at weekends.

TASK

C Divide the class into two. Hold a debate on the motion: "Taxes will be increased *heavily* so that our country can give more money to Third World Development programmes."

Half the class supports this "Government" proposal. The other half opposes it.

ISSUE 11 MONEY AND POSSESSIONS

What do Christians Think?

Members of the early Christian community shared what they had with each other. Jesus had made it clear in his teaching that when people try to serve God generously, money and possessions could get in the way.

Here are six examples of that teaching of Jesus.

Read the texts in full.

TASK

Work in groups to see if you can give examples which illustrate each of the six texts.
e.g. (for C) Cocaine barons who build up empires for themselves.
(for F) Missionaries like Mother Teresa who overcome the difficulty and accept a life of poverty.

Matthew 6:19-34

A The Sermon on the Mount

Wealth gets in the way.

"You cannot serve both God and money."

Luke 12:13-21

B The Parable of the Rich Fool

"A person's true life is not made up of the things he owns, no matter how rich he may be."

Luke 16:19-31

C The Parable of the Rich Man and Lazarus

Wealth can make people think only of themselves.

Matthew 6:1-4

D Giving money away quietly

"When you give something to a needy person, do not make a big show of it...."

Mark 12:41-44

E The Widow's Offering

Real generosity is giving away as much as you can.

Mark 10:17-31

F The Rich Man

It is difficult for wealthy people to swap their life style for one of poverty in the service of God and neighbour.

Work for your Folder

TASKS

1

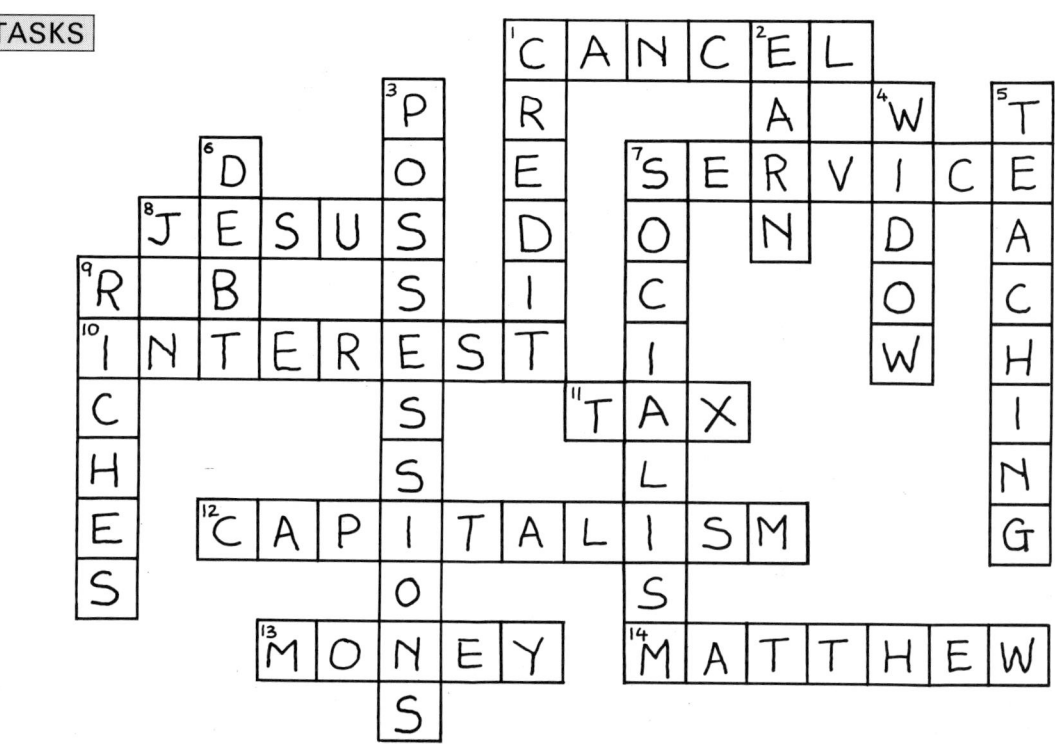

▶ Here are the answers to a word-puzzle on MONEY.
All these words are used in the text (pages 44–46).

ACROSS	DOWN
1........	1........
7........	2........
8........	3........
10........	4........
11........	5........
12........	6........
13........	7........
14........	9........

▶ Using the text, write clues that would get these answers.

Example:
1 DOWN The name of cards that allow you to buy NOW, pay later.

2 Write out the Parable of the Rich Man and Lazarus.
Better still—type it out.

▶ Stick it on a piece of coloured card/paper.

▶ Use the results of the group task on page 46 to illustrate it.

▶ Copy the summary of the story from page 46 (see illustration).

▶ Repeat this with another one of the six texts.

ISSUE 12
Addiction

"Do you smoke?"
"I thought it was BIG to start smoking. Now I know it was a BIG MISTAKE."

Kirsty, Aged 15

▶ Get into groups of four.
Make a list of the reasons why you think people START to smoke.

1 ....
2 ....
3 ....
4 ....
5 ....

CHECK

Interview 5 people you know who smoke. Ask them *how* they came to start.

One person in every four will die early from smoking-related diseases. It could be one person in your group.

Secondary smoking:
It is believed that people can die from other people's smoking. The air is polluted with poisonous carbon monoxide.

Today more and more public places ban smoking or have only a small area set aside for smokers.

▶ *List* the public places that ban or control smoking.

▶ Write a letter to the press complaining that you want to be FREE to smoke.

▶ Write another letter as if you were objecting to the first letter.

Footballer Duncan Forbes joins the campaign

TASKS

1 Design a slogan for a T-shirt as part of an anti-smoking campaign. Can you do better than the one designed and printed at Sprowston High School (see previous column)?

2 It takes a lot of character to resist smoking if friends smoke. It requires for example, SELF-CONTROL.
List other qualities it requires.

"Have another drink!"

Alcohol blamed
By Jill Sherman, Social Services Correspondent

Almost half of all accidental deaths in teenagers aged over 15 are caused by alcohol, according to the Royal College of Psychiatrists. Alcohol is to blame for 45 percent of fatal road accidents involving young people and is also linked to other accidents such as drowning and accidental suicide. "An alcohol overdose with or without other drugs is commonplace" the Royal College said yesterday.

A discussion paper, to be published today, warns that the effect of alcohol on driving skills is much greater amongst inexperienced drivers. Driving competence declines in most drivers above a blood alcohol level of 80 milligrams but in inexperienced drivers deteriorates after 50mg.

A recent national survey of children aged 13 to 17 showed that 26 percent of those aged 13 in England and Wales reported drinking alcohol three or more days the previous week.

- Remember that getting drunk doesn't make you tall, rich, strong, handsome, smart, witty, sophisticated or sexy.

Alcohol is a serious problem. Wine, beer and spirits are so easy to buy that people don't realize they are buying an addictive drug. There are no serious health warnings on the labels as there are on packets of cigarettes.

Amazing Statistics
During the time this lesson takes (single period) the Government will collect about £½ million on alcohol TAX (i.e. £200 per second).

During this same period the Government will spend £240 on campaigns to control drinking (i.e. 10p per second).

CLASS TASK
1 Make a depressing collage from newspaper cuttings, magazines and your own drawings to show the misery that alcohol can bring.

2 When it is finished discuss whether it is an unfair comment on alcohol. Is there not some good to be said for it?

ALCOHOLICS ANONYMOUS
was founded in 1935 by a New York business man and an Ohio doctor. They had both been addicted to alcohol. They devised a "12 steps" plan for alcoholics to follow in an attempt to break the addiction. One of the 12 steps states:

"We have made a decision to turn our wills and our lives over to the care of God as we understand him."

What do Christians Think?

Most Christians see alcohol, used in moderation, as a gift from God. Wine is a central part of most Eucharist Services (though some denominations use unfermented wine). It is the misuse of alcohol and other drugs that they deplore.

They regard the human body as sacred, the "temple of the Holy Spirit" (1 Corinthians 6:19–20).

They believe they are not free to misuse their bodies, and are concerned about the damage addicts do to themselves, and to others.

What others?   And what damage?

Fr. Dunstan Thill is one of many Christians who have set up rehabilitation centres for addicts

Drugs can destroy or distort the human mind.
Drugs can damage the body.
Drugs can kill.

Christians are also concerned about the causes of addiction. In some cases addiction results from:

> unemployment,
> broken marriage,
> rape,
> mental breakdown,
> death of a loved one.

Christians try to act with compassion for the victims of drug and alcohol abuse, and their families. Just as Jesus acted with compassion to the victims of his society.

> "Show me someone who drinks too much, ... and I will show you someone miserable and sorry for himself and always causing trouble...."
> Proverbs 23:29

▶ What values and beliefs do you think underlie the Christian attitude towards drug-taking?

Work for your Folder

1 Cut out a cigarette advert from a magazine. Redesign the same advert to say the opposite—that is, to DISCOURAGE smoking.

2 Design a logo for Alcoholics Anonymous.
▶ Copy the information about A.A. (page 49) on to a sheet of file paper.
▶ Decorate the page with your logo.
▶ Can you find out the local address of the organization?
Add it to your A.A. page.

3
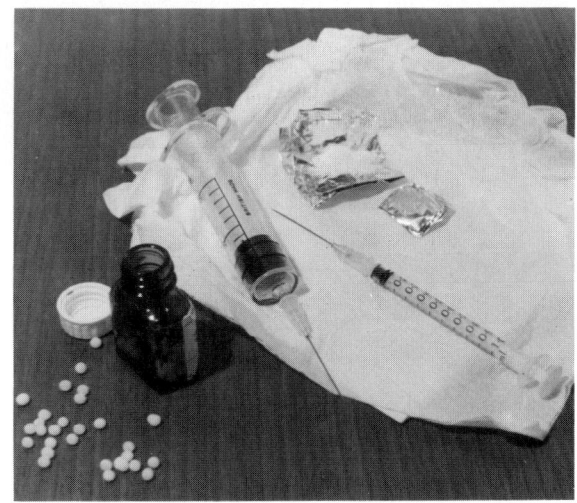

You have just discovered that your brother is taking drugs. Write down:
a what you are going to do,
b what you might say to him.

Do you think a Christian would write down anything different from a non-Christian?
If so, what, and why?
If not, why not?

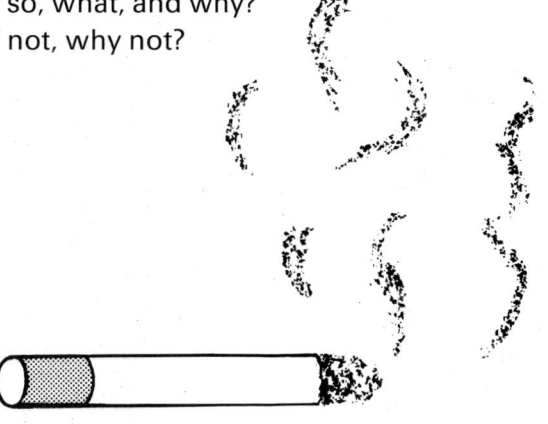

4 Write to A.S.H. for information about the organization.
   A.S.H.,
   (Action on Smoking and Health,)
   5–11 Mortimer Street,
   London W1N 7RH.

Start an anti-smoking campaign in your school.
Find a member of the staff to help you.
Plan an assembly with her/him.
Make posters.

ISSUE 13

Evil, Crime and the Law

Why do people turn to crime?

Eight prisoners were asked why they had committed their crime.
These are the replies:

1 "Because I hated the man. He had taken my wife from me."
2 "Well, if you had lost your job and got into debt, what would you have done?"
3 "I hang around all day with nothing to do. So I got in with this crowd...."
4 "I'm a single parent. When I've paid the rent and fed the kids I have no money for clothes. I have to shoplift to get anything nice."
5 "I don't know. I have these voices in my head telling me to do things."
6 "I want to live in luxury. I nearly got away with it."
7 "I hate these foreigners. We've too many of them about."
8 "I needed the money for drugs."

Here are eight *causes* of crime identified by social workers:
A Unemployment
B Greed
C Boredom
D Poverty
E Prejudice
F Addiction
G Sickness
H Revenge

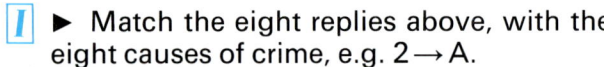

▶ Match the eight replies above, with the eight causes of crime, e.g. 2 → A.

▶ Make up eight *situations* which could lead to crime. Each situation must have a different cause. Here is the first one done for you.

A Unemployment
Roy, aged 49, lost his job. He wrote over 30 letters in reply to adverts. He never even got one interview. He visited the job centre daily. Nothing. One day he threw a brick through its window.

How would you treat offenders?

Wayne is serving a long prison sentence for manslaughter.

At 15 he got hooked on drugs after experimenting at a friend's party.

He began stealing to pay for his drugs.

He even stole from his parents.

By 18, he was very ill and he discovered he had the AIDS virus.

Shocked at this discovery he went and got drunk.

Wayne doesn't remember driving home that night.

He knocked down a young woman. She died.

Why do you think Wayne is being punished?

A TO PROTECT SOCIETY
"These addicts are a menace. Now they are giving us AIDS too. They need to be locked away from us." ANNE

B FOR REVENGE
"He should have been given a death sentence. He killed our daughter. Why should he live?" TOM

C TO DETER OTHERS FROM CRIME
"We need long sentences for people like Wayne. Then people will think twice before going on drugs or drink." BILL

D TO REFORM HIM
"One silly experiment with drugs has led to all this misery. Wayne needs help to rebuild his life." PAT

TASKS

1 ▶ With whom do you have most sympathy, Anne, Tom, Bill or Pat?
Write A, B, C, D on the board and take a class vote.

▶ Perhaps prison punishes people for all four reasons.
Write A, B, C, D in what you think is the order of importance, (e.g. If you want *most* of all to deter others, put C first.)

▶ Which one did you put last? Would you want to drop it altogether?

G ▶ Get into groups. Compare answers. Defend your answer to your group.

ISSUE 13 EVIL, CRIME AND THE LAW

What do Christians Think?

A letter from Mary to her friend.

> Rose Cottage
> Country Lane
> Blythe.
>
> Dear Sarah,
>
> You'll never guess what's happened. Sam has come home. Mum has welcomed him with open arms — and after all he did to her. She must have gone off her head!
>
> You remember how he left home after that row. We were worried sick. Not a word for a year and then it was the police who came round. He had been picked up with a fighting crowd after a football match. He was living in a squat and in a terrible mess.
>
> You'll remember how Mum cried and cried when Sam refused to come home. He said he wanted his freedom.
>
> He turned up last night. Mum is treating him as though he never hurt her. In fact I'm quite fed up with the whole

Read Luke 15:11–32
Luke says that Jesus told the story of The Lost Son to show how God always forgives the sinner (offender).

This is, for many Christians, the most important teaching in their religion.

It is likely that most Christians would want to help offenders and not seek revenge.

Work for your Folder

Christians believe that if they look at Jesus they will see what God is like.

1 Look up the following text in Luke's Gospel and choose someone to read it aloud to the group or class.

Luke 5 : 29–32
Write out this summary:

> **Luke 5 : 29–32** Jesus is happy to mix with outcasts and sinners.
>
> "I have not come to call respectable people to repent but outcasts."   Verse 32

2 Repeat this exercise with the following texts. When you write the summaries complete the quotations.

> **Luke 6 : 27–38** Jesus invites people to forgive one another completely.
>
> "Love your enemies, ..."   Verse 27

> **Luke 9 : 51–56** Jesus tells his friends off for seeking revenge.
>
> "When the disciples . . . ."   Verses 54, 55

> **Luke 15 : 1–7** Jesus says that God is overjoyed when a sinner repents.
>
> "In the same way . . . ."   Verse 7

> **Luke 23 : 32–41** Jesus forgives even those who kill him unjustly.
>
> "Jesus said, '. . . .'"   Verse 34

3 From these texts would you say that God forgives EVERY person no matter what sin or crime has been committed?

4 Invite a local prison chaplain to come and talk with your class.

ISSUE 14
Politics and International Affairs

CHRISTIANITY AND WAR

War veterans keep up the memory of those who died for our freedom

Is a ceremony like the one in the photograph a celebration of war or of peace?

Some people say it would be better to forgive and forget the past. What do you think? What do some Christians think?

> "All Christians agree that war is evil. Some believe that it is, therefore, in every circumstance to be rejected by the follower of Christ. Others believe that there are situations in which waging of war is inevitable as the choice of the lesser of two admitted evils."
>
> *Methodist* statement on *Peace and War. Declaration and Statements.*

This statement points out that there is more than one view.

VIEW 1

The Quakers Peace Testimony

... We testify to the world that the spirit of Christ, which leads us into all truth, will never move us to fight and war against any man with outward weapons, neither for the kingdom of

"Some believe that it is in every circumstance to be rejected by the follower of Christ."

People who believe that fighting is *not* the way to win freedom are called PACIFISTS.

Some Christians claim that Jesus was a Pacifist. The Quakers (Society of Friends) are a Christian group who are totally pacifist.

VIEW 2

Peace priest

Defiant priest Fr Daniel McAvoy has stated his readiness to go to prison rather than pay a fine for his act of civil disobedience at the Ministry of Defence, Whitehall on Ash Wednesday.
He is among 39 Christians who will be in the dock facing charges of criminal damage later this month and into the next. All have stated their intention to plead not guilty and to provide their own defence for actions which received the support of two Anglican bishops and Auxiliary Bishop Victor Guazzelli of East London last March 4.

Many Christians take the view that it is wrong not only to use nuclear weapons, but even to *possess* them. Some Christians, like Fr. McAvoy belong to Christian C.N.D. (Campaign for Nuclear Disarmament).

> "Modern weapons of war are evidence of madness. Society is spending its best brains and much of its budget on planning the lunatic unthinkable."   Dr. Robert Runcie

VIEW 3

"Others believe that there are situations in which waging of war is inevitable as the choice of the lesser of two evils."

The army chaplain will accept this view.

> So will those who support the JUST WAR theory. This says that a war can be fought, under strict conditions:
> It must be started by recognized authority,
> be for a just cause,
> have a right intention (e.g. peace),
> be a last resort,
> always protect civilians,
> control behaviour of troops.

Work for your Folder

1 Choose one quotation from these pages. Make it the centre-piece of a *large* poster or collage for a school corridor.

2 Write out and complete the following sentences:

a The Quakers are Pacifists. This means they believe that....

b Dr. Runcie said (about nuclear weapons), "....

c C.N.D. means....

d Mahatma Ghandi once said, "....

e A *just war* is one which fulfils the following six conditions, (i) ....

3 Under what conditions, if any, would you be prepared to fight in a war? For example, if people were treated unjustly, with no other way of receiving just treatment?

> "For the price of one jet fighter (about £20 million) one could set up 40,000 village pharmacies." *Brandt Report.*

> "In the Third World someone dies of starvation every fifteen seconds. But every fifteen seconds the nations of the world are spending £75,000 preparing for the next war (which neither side can win).
> Lord Macleod in *Unholy Warfare.*

> "An eye for an eye and we shall soon all be blind"
> (Mahatma Ghandi)

ISSUE 14 POLITICS AND INTERNATIONAL AFFAIRS

CHRISTIANITY AND POLITICS

The Church in the British Isles

Here are what six people have said about the Church and Politics:

1 "The Church's primary role must be a spiritual one. I speak as an Anglican."
Patrick Jenkin, M.P.

2 "The Head of the Church of England is the Queen. There are bishops in the House of Lords. So the Church must be taking part in politics." Karl, aged 12

3 "To be political, when it has to do with justice and the common good, is a duty laid down by the Gospel."
Fr. Patrick O'Mahoney, R.C. priest

4 "Didn't Jesus say, 'My Kingdom is not of this world'? Why do Church people, like the Bishop of Durham, tell the Government what they ought to be doing? They should shut up." Sheila, aged 51

5 "The way that you can destroy the Christian faith is to distort Christ's words and make his kingdom of this world. This is what many elements in the Churches are doing."
Malcolm Muggeridge

6 "We urge an increasing number of Catholics to seek active roles in the vast field of central and local government."
R.C. National Pastoral Conference

Was Jesus a political figure?

TASKS

1 The statements show two points of view.
  1 Write the six statements out under the headings:
     a The Church must avoid politics,
     b The Church must be political.
  (There are three statements in each group.)

  2 Which side would you support? Why?

The Church in the World

When Archbishop Desmond Tutu of Johannesburg was told "Don't mix religion with politics," he replied:

> "Does it say anywhere that God is not interested too much in what happens from Monday to Saturday but only in what happens on Sunday?"

Archbishop Tutu works peacefully for people deprived of justice and human rights in South Africa. Some Christians have even felt the need to enter into violent confrontation with corrupt authorities.

Father Camilo Torres lived and died for the poor Colombian shanty-town dwellers

Life of Father Camilo Torres
- **Born 1930**
in Colombia, South America.
- He became a Roman Catholic priest in Bogotà, the capital city.
- He believed that being a Christian meant being concerned for his neighbour.
- His neighbours were poor people who were treated unjustly by rich land owners.
- He wanted to work peacefully to bring to the poor a share of their country's wealth.
- The Government responded harshly with force.
- He received no support from the official Catholic Church.
- He had to choose between his cause and his priesthood.
- He stopped being a priest and became a revolutionary leader.
- **Died 1966**
- Killed in fighting for peasants against Government troops.

TASKS

▶ Find out about Martin Luther King, who was also killed for standing alongside the oppressed. But he preached *non-violence*.

▶ In groups discuss the two responses to injustice.

ISSUE 15

Environment

"The earth has enough for every man's need, but not for every man's greed."   Ghandi

Destruction of the rainforests—many life-saving plants are being destroyed along with the trees

In order to live we need food, water, fresh air, medicines, warmth, shelter and means of power. The earth provides us with all these needs. But the earth's NATURAL RESOURCES are limited.

We are using them up too quickly and we are misusing them. In fact, our misuse of resources is becoming a huge problem. It is causing as much international concern as the nuclear arms issue.

Politicians have been slow to act but there is now a growing political movement in Europe called The Green Party. Its members are concerned for the conservation of the earth.

TASKS

1 Make a list of all the ways in which the earth's resources are being destroyed.
▶ Compare your list with your neighbours'. (Keep your results.)

2 Search the newspapers/magazines for cuttings about the destruction or pollution of the earth's resources. Keep these in a class folder for future use.

3 Write to one of these groups working for conservation for information about environmental issues.
Display the information.
GREENPEACE,
36 Graham Street, London N1 8LL.
FRIENDS OF THE EARTH,
9 Poland Street, London W1 3DG.
WORLD WIDE FUND FOR NATURE,
Panda House, Weyside Park, Goldalming, Surrey GU7 1XR.
SURVIVAL INTERNATIONAL,
36 Craven Street, London WC2.
THE PEOPLE'S TRUST FOR ENDANGERED SPECIES,
Meadrow, Godalming, Surrey GU7 3JX.

WWF World Wide Fund For Nature

What do Christians Think?

In the Jewish/Christian creation poem (Genesis 1) God puts the earth into the hands of human beings.

Christians use the Jewish prayers, the Psalms, to express their joy over the whole of creation.

> "Lord, you have made so many things! How wisely you made them all!"
> Psalm 104:24

Christians believe that God's world is spoilt by greed and selfishness. In the past, many Christians thought natural disasters, like floods or earthquakes, were deliberately sent by God to punish people. Today most Christians recognize that human beings can cause even these "natural" disasters by their selfish misuse of the land.

In recent years Christians have come to respect the wisdom of ancient tribal peoples. Missionaries used to call their ideas "superstitions". Today Christians listen to them more readily. They recognize that Aborigines and American Indians, for example, have a magnificent sense of harmony with the earth.

> "This we know—the earth does not belong to the people, the people belong to the earth. Whatever happens to the earth happens to the children of the earth. People did not weave the web of life; they are merely strands in it. Whatever they do to the web, they do to themselves."
> Chief Seattle, North American Indian

Some Things to Do

1 What are natural disasters?
▶ In what way can people cause these disasters by misuse of the land?
▶ Do you think we should feel in any way responsible for future generations?

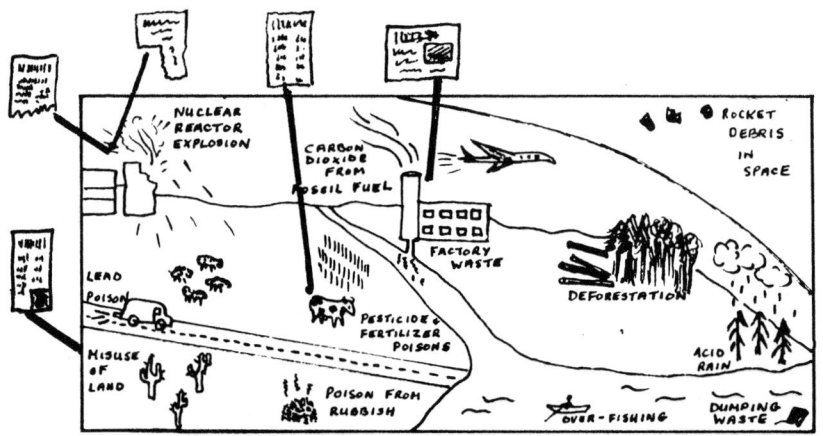

2 *Work in a group.* Draw this chart on a large scale as a poster about 1 metre × ½ metre.
▶ Using the newspaper cuttings you collected (TASK 2, page 60) pin them around your poster and use ribbons to connect them with the drawing. (See example above.)

Collect up crisp packets etc. dropped on a school field or drive.
STICK or PIN onto a large sheet of paper and display in the corridor. Ask the question:
"If today's school-field litter took up 2 m × 1 m space, how much space will it take up in a term?"

3 An idea for a litter campaign.

Some Things to Do

1

"O Lord, our Lord,
Your greatness is seen in all the world! . . . .
When I look at the sky, which you have made,
At the moon and the stars, which you set in their places—
What is man, that you think of him? . . . ."

Psalm 8

CLASS TASK

▶ Do you think human beings are the best part of creation? Give reasons for your answer.
▶ Read Psalm 104.
▶ Find a photograph (one of your own if you are a photographer) of a part of creation that appeals to you—birds, mountains, fish, trees etc.

▶ Stick your photo on to a sheet of A4 paper and write alongside the appropriate part of Psalm 104.
▶ Display the results.
▶ To develop this theme find a poem (in the English library?) which would also illustrate your photo.

2

Read Genesis 6:9 – 7:23
▶ Discuss why the People's Trust, which is concerned for endangered animals, has chosen the ark symbol for its organization.
▶ Write out a brief account of the story of Noah.
▶ Mount it on the corner of a sheet of paper/card.
▶ Draw a large boat and add endangered animals.
▶ Collect information from the PEOPLE'S TRUST to add to the chart.

Index

Aborigines 61
Abortion 14
  Law Reform Association 14
Addictions 48–51
  alcohol 49
  drugs 50
  smoking 48
Adoption 13
AGE CONCERN 25
Alcohol addiction 49
ALCOHOLICS ANONYMOUS 49
American Indians 61
ASH 51

Borrowing 44
Brandt Report 57

CAFOD 30
Capitalism 44
CATHOLIC CHILDREN'S SOCIETY 14
Children 12–15
CHRISTIAN AID 30, 34
Christians 3
Colour and prejudice 18
Communion 33
Contraception 12
Creation 5
Credit cards 44
Crime 52–55
CYRENIANS 31

Death 26
Debt 45
Discrimination 18
DR. BARNARDO'S 14

Ecumenism 18
Educating the world 34. 35
Environment 60–63
Eucharist 33, 50
Evil 52

Family 4–7
  patterns 4
Feeding the world 32, 33
First World 32
Forgiveness 7, 55
Fostering 13
Friends 4–7
FRIENDS OF THE EARTH 60

Green Party 60
GREENPEACE 60

Handicap 20–23
Healing 29
HELP THE AGED 25
Hospice movement 26
Hospitals 24
Housing 28
Human rights 59

Interest 44
International affairs 56–59
Investment 44

Justice 59

L'ARCHE 21, 23
Law 52–55
Leisure 40–43
  as an industry 41
LIFE 14
Litter 62
Love 8

Marriage 8–11
  Christian marriage 10
  monogamy 11
  sex in marriage 10
  vows 10
MENCAP 23
Mental handicap 21
Missionaries 24
  Medical Missionaries of Mary 29, 31
Money 44–47
Mystery of death 26, 27

Natural disasters 62
Natural resources 60
Non-violence 59
Nursing 24

Offenders 53
Old Age 25
One-World Week 33

Pacifists 56
Pain 24
Paradise 26
PEOPLE'S TRUST FOR ENDANGERED SPECIES 60, 63
PHAB 23
Physical handicap 20
Politics 58–59
  and Jesus 58
  and the Church 59

Pollution 62
Possessions 44–47
Prejudice 16–19
  and colour 18
  and Jesus 58
  and race 18
  and religion 18
  and sex 18
  and the Church 59
Problems 6

Quakers and peace 56, 57

Race and prejudice 18
Recreation 41
Religion and politics 58, 59
  and prejudice 18

Salary 44
SAMARITANS 28, 31
Scapegoats 16, 17
Sex and prejudice 18
SHELTER 31
Smoking 48
Socialism 44
ST. JOHN'S AMBULANCE BRIGADE 24
Sunday 42
Surrogacy 13
SURVIVAL INTERNATIONAL 60

Test-tube babies 13
Third World 32
  debt 45
  hunger 57
  work in 36
Trade Unions 36

UN declaration 22
Unemployment 36–39

Vatican II 5

Wage 44
War 56, 57
  Just 57
  Methodist statement 56
  Nuclear 56
Weddings 9
Work 36–39
WORLD WILD FUND FOR NATURE 60